Building on God's Foundation

1999—2000 NWMS READING BOOKS

RESOURCE BOOK FOR THE LEADER
IMAGINE THE FUTURE
Edited by Beverlee Borbe

FOR THE READER

BEHIND THE SILENCE
The Story of Frank and Ann Sutherland
By Robert Sutherland and John Sutherland

BUILDING ON GOD'S FOUNDATION
50 Years of Alabaster
Edited by Tim Crutcher

JUST AROUND THE CORNER
Compassion in San Bernardino
By Robin Hyde as told to Cynthia Sherer

LOYD AND NITA MARTZ
Pioneers in Volunteer Missions
By Lela Morgan

PORTUGAL: A PLACE OF REFUGE
By Maria João Guerreiro

THROUGH HIS EYES
The Story of Youth in Mission
Edited by Ken Couchman and Jason E. Vickers

BUILDING ON GOD'S FOUNDATION

50 YEARS OF ALABASTER

EDITED BY TIM CRUTCHER

Nazarene Publishing House
Kansas City, Missouri

To the memory of
Rev. Estelle Crutcher
and
Dr. Earl Lee
who left me a family heritage
beyond price
and an example of faith
for which I shall ever be grateful.

Contents

Tim Crutcher and his wife, Rhonda, serve as
Nazarenes In Volunteer Service (NIVS) in Belgium.
Tim, a former mission education coordinator for NWMS,
is a freelance writer.

Foreword

GOD ALWAYS HAS HIS PLAN—His *idea*—to build the Kingdom. He is interested in every detail, including buildings. While it is true that the church is not dependent upon buildings, they certainly are vital to a congregation's ministry and outreach.

Alabaster is one of the *God-ideas*, given to our denomination through Rev. Elizabeth Vennum, that has enabled the Church of the Nazarene to help provide buildings and property—churches, schools, clinics and hospitals, homes, and offices—for our mission endeavors. As a missionary worker on the field for 24 years, I saw the incredible value of the Alabaster fund. Sometimes we would use Alabaster money as a *seed* to help a local congregation "grow" its own buildings. Other times the Alabaster fund enabled us to build an entire church, so that a congregation could begin to meet. As I witnessed the spending of Alabaster dollars, I was constantly reminded of this *God-idea* to build His Church. He has used the people called Nazarenes to expand and multiply His Church through Alabaster giving.

The sacrificial giving of Nazarenes over the years has enabled the Alabaster fund to be used like the ointment in an alabaster container that was broken and poured out upon Jesus' feet. Like that love gift, many Nazarenes have literally given up something of value to be able to put money—their love gift—into the Alabaster Offering. This exemplary selflessness is indicative of our people who desire to help build His Church—to be a part of the *God-idea*.

Consider what Alabaster funds have accomplished since its inception in 1949:

Churches and chapels	2,392
Educational institutions	265
Hospitals and clinics	34
Missionary homes	277
National workers' homes	852
Mission and district centers	146
Land/property	970
Miscellaneous	603
TOTAL	5,539

In the 21st century, Alabaster will continue to be one of the significant tools God will use to help Nazarenes construct necessary buildings. Through our worldwide evangelism program, using the "Each One Win One" plan and the JESUS Film Partnership, we will see millions won to Christ. This, of course, will necessitate hundreds—yea, thousands—of new buildings. I challenge you to join me, through your Alabaster gifts, in supporting this great evangelistic thrust. And I invite you to celebrate with me in being a part of the *God-idea* called Alabaster.

—Louie E. Bustle
World Mission Division Director

Acknowledgments

ALL COLLECTIONS OF STORIES, such as this one, are dependent upon the creative energies and dedication of far more people than those whose names are found on the cover. As editor of this collection, I would like to acknowledge the creative efforts of the following who helped this book become reality: Rev. Elizabeth Vennum, Dr. Curtis Lewis Jr., Rev. Steve and Jean Hazelton, Rev. Al Swain, Rev. Robert McCroskey Jr., Rev. Leonel de Leon Vega, and Mrs. Diane Barker. I am also indebted to the generous hospitality of Rev. Trevor and Mary Johnston. And finally, I am grateful to all the Nazarenes who have ever given to Alabaster, for without your generosity there would be nothing to tell.

Introduction

WHAT A LONG AND EXHAUSTING DAY it had been! The wind whipping around the hill where Jesus had been teaching had tied our hair into knots. Philip and I wondered if we would ever get the grit out of our teeth. Even Matthew, who was normally very proper with his appearance, looked disheveled. All of us were looking forward to what we felt was a well-deserved time of relaxation and what ought to be a delicious meal.

One of the local religious leaders named Simon had invited Jesus to dinner that evening. And as always, the 12 of us tagged along. Pharisees didn't always make the best of company, but then I've heard some people say the same about Jesus too. Jesus seemed very willing to go, and that didn't leave us much choice. So, we did our best to look presentable, arrived at the appropriate time, and took our places, reclining on worn but comfortable cushions. As usual, the "Thunder Boys" nabbed the spots closest to Jesus, but this one time the rest of us didn't mind. The food looked scrumptious, and after a week of hard bread and fish, we were ready for a change.

We had just taken our places and the dinner was about to start when a woman entered the room from the side closest to the street. I think Andrew saw her first, and he pointed her out to me. The first thing I noticed was that she was crying. She was dressed in a tattered robe that at one time probably had been quite nice but was now showing its age. Philip commented he thought she had been one of the people in the crowd earlier that day, but he couldn't be sure. She was plain and unremarkable, except for her hair. She had dark, flowing tresses, almost down to her waist.

Within a few moments, everyone in the room was staring at her. She avoided their puzzled and unfriendly gazes as best she could as her tearful eyes scanned the room, eventually coming to rest on Jesus. Then she made a beeline for Him. If Jesus noticed her, He didn't let it show but calmly continued His conversation with our host. As the woman made her way through the room, hushed whispers followed her. Apparently everyone in town knew who she was. Reclining as I was away from Jesus and closer to the other guests at the table, I was able to make out a few words. The one that came up most often was *harlot*.

It wasn't until she was almost right behind Jesus that our host finally noticed this new guest. He stopped midsentence, and I could see his head turn from Jesus to the woman, then back and forth again. Jesus, however, didn't even look. Most of the other guests had stopped talking. They tried to observe everything without it being obvious. They didn't have long to wait.

Now, I don't know if that woman knew she had an audience, but she acted as if no one else in the world existed except her and Jesus. She knelt down behind Him close to His feet, fumbling with something tied at her waist. Still crying, she bent over to untie whatever it was she had brought with her, and her tears began to fall on Jesus' feet.

She bent down, kissed Jesus' feet, and lavishly poured the entire contents of the jar on them.

She finally worked free a bag from her belt and pulled out a container of something or other. The jar looked to be made of alabaster, so whatever it contained must have been valuable. As she opened the jar, she must have noticed that her tears had pretty much soaked Jesus' feet, because she began looking around. Apparently not finding what she was looking for, she began to dry His feet with the only thing available to her—her hair.

Then she broke open the jar she was carrying, and soon all of us smelled the most wonderful fragrance. Then she did something I will never forget. She bent down, kissed Jesus' feet, and lavishly poured the entire contents of the jar on them. For some reason this made her cry even more, and she bent down to kiss His feet again.

We all watched in amazement. For some of us, it was that ceaseless wonder at the effect Jesus seemed to have on people. For others, however, I could tell it was shock. I heard Judas scornfully speak to Thaddaeus, "What a waste! She could have sold that perfume for a lot of money and given it to the poor. Now half of it has been lost on the floor."

The hushed whispers around me started up again, and I heard people wondering why Simon didn't have "that vulgar woman" thrown out of his house. Simon, our host, seemed to be the most appalled of all and began to cast doubting looks in Jesus' direction. It was as if Simon could not believe Jesus was so unaware of the kind of woman touching Him and kissing His feet.

For the first time Jesus looked down at the woman. She was still crying at His feet, though more softly now. She continued to keep her eyes cast down and seemed unwilling to look directly at Him. Perhaps she was embarrassed by her exuberant display. Perhaps she had realized all the eyes in the room were on her. I don't know. Jesus smiled that kind and gentle smile of His and turned back to our host. The hushed whispers quickly died away as Jesus spoke to Simon, just loud enough to be heard by everyone in the room.

"Simon, let me tell you something."

Simon was obviously disconcerted and had no idea what to make of the situation. Still, he noticed that everyone was now looking at him, and he knew how to play to the crowd. Regaining a measure of control, he said in his most self-assured voice, "Speak, Rabbi." And that Jesus most certainly did.

"There was a banker," Jesus said, "who had two people who owed him money. The first one owed him about 18 months' earnings, the second about 2 months' worth. Times being what they were, neither of these people could pay their debt. The banker was a generous man, and when he learned of this, he canceled both of their debts. Now, which of them do you think would love him more?"

Not sure where all this was leading, Simon hesitated, then eventually answered, "I suppose the one for whom he canceled the greater debt."

Jesus smiled again. "Exactly," He said. Turning to the woman, but with His voice still directed at Simon, He asked, "Do you see this woman?"

Simon gave a look that said, *How could I possibly have missed her!*

"When I arrived this evening," Jesus continued, "you offered Me no water to wash away the dirt of the street. But this woman has bathed My feet with her tears and dried them with her hair."

I noticed a small flush rising in Simon's face, but Jesus went on relentlessly. "You gave Me no kiss of greeting, but from the time I came in here this woman has not stopped kissing My feet. You did not anoint My head with oil, but she has anointed My feet with this wonderful perfume.

"Now, let Me tell you that her sins, which you certainly know are numerous, have all been forgiven. That is why she has made this great display of love and affection. She knows what she has been saved from. Others who've only been forgiven a little seem only to love a little in return."

Then Jesus reached over to the woman and gently raised her head with His hand. He looked deeply at her with those compelling eyes of His and said, "Your sins are forgiven. It was your faith that made it happen. Now, go and be at peace."

At those words, the guests began to whisper again. "Who is this man that even forgives sins? What kind of person is Jesus anyway?"

The woman, however, probably heard none of these things. She got up slowly, never taking her eyes from Jesus. Then she smiled. It was one of the most beautiful smiles I've ever seen. Then her eyes slowly and deliberately scanned around the room again. This time, it was the guests who looked away. She smoothed the folds of her robe and unhurriedly made her way to the door. She couldn't have been a rich woman, but at that moment, she looked as if she owned the world. Whatever the value was of that perfume she had "wasted" on Jesus, she looked as if she had gained infinitely more.

✳ ✳ ✳

This familiar and probing story from the life of Christ (adapted from Luke 7:36-50) is the basis for the Alabaster program in the Church of the Nazarene. In this book, you are invited to take a glimpse into just a few ways Alabaster has made and continues to make a difference, turning momentary sacrifices into eternal rewards.

CHAPTER 1

Building the Alabaster Foundation

ELIZABETH VENNUM LAY IN HER BERTH, listening to the clickety-clack of the train speeding over the rails. The sound was rhythmic, comforting, and restful, a sharp contrast to the hard work of several days of meetings. January is never the best time to visit Kansas City, and when one hails from the balmy climes of southern Florida, making the trip to attend council meetings is no small sacrifice. She had even come down with the flu for her troubles, thanks no doubt to the wretched Kansas City winters. The past few days she had been too sick even to think about the assignment the council had given her, and the gentle rocking of the train was encouraging her to put off such thinking again in favor of much-needed sleep and warm dreams of the Miami sunshine still a couple of days away.

Yet Rev. Vennum was not one to let such troubles as committees or sickness get her down. She enjoyed serving on the General Council for the Women's Foreign Missionary Society (WFMS), which is now the Nazarene World Mission Society (NWMS), of the Church of the Nazarene. She made the yearly trips joyfully and counted her troubles as small sacrifices compared to those of the missionaries she worked to support. It was, in fact, one of those missionary *troubles* that had prompted the assignment she had been given.

A serious crisis in giving for missions existed in the church in those days, even though the country had recovered well in the two and a half years since the end of World War II. Perhaps there was a mistrust of all things foreign, since their children and siblings had gone off to fight in Germany or the Pacific, many of whom didn't come home. Perhaps President Truman's warnings about the growth of Communism made people feel their resources were better spent at home. Whatever the reason, the money that had come in for missions during the previous year in 1947 would not be enough to meet all the needs for the current year, especially when it came to providing the needed buildings—churches and hospitals and schools and houses—to carry out the work of the Kingdom. The General WFMS Council had asked Elizabeth to submit a plan within six months that would help increase missionary giving. It was a strong challenge, but then Elizabeth knew her God was good at meeting such challenges.

As the train rumbled on, Elizabeth voiced the same short petition she had prayed in her room in Kansas City a day or so before. "Lord, You know Your servant, and You know this assignment. If You can use my mind to think through and my heart to love through, I'm available."

As Elizabeth sat there, praying and reading her Bible, she sensed the Lord directing her thoughts.

Rev. Elizabeth Vennum

She felt drawn to the story of the woman who had poured out the expensive alabaster jar of perfume on Jesus. If ever there had been a selfless offering, that was one. The more she pondered the event, the more she felt a growing warmth in her own heart. *How wonderful*, she thought, *to have had the opportunity to give Jesus himself such a gift, to demonstrate love for Him in such a tangible manner!*

Elizabeth imagined herself in that woman's place; but when she looked at Jesus, she saw Him reaching down into dark places on the earth and lifting up the poor and needy to sit beside Him. *Do you really want to do something for Me?* she sensed Him asking. "*Inasmuch as ye have done it unto one of the least of these my brethren, ye have done it unto me*" (Matt. 25:40, KJV).

The God-inspired idea would evoke the power and fervor of the biblical alabaster sacrifice.

Overwhelmed, Elizabeth heard that scripture verse echo again and again in her mind. She knew that if Jesus himself had come to her or any of the members of her church, they would give Him whatever He asked, whatever He needed. They would gladly sacrifice just for the privilege of giving something to Jesus in person. Slowly and forcefully the full weight of that scripture imprinted itself on her heart. Jesus was indeed here in person, and gifts given to the least of His children count as gifts given personally to Him.

Gradually, the details of a giving plan began to take shape in Elizabeth's mind. The God-inspired idea would evoke the power and fervor of the biblical alabaster sacrifice and remind all Nazarenes of the privilege they have in giving to Jesus in person—through His needy children around the world.

She took out a pen and notepad from her suitcase and began to jot down details of the plan as they came to her. She saw small alabaster-like boxes in Nazarene homes, boxes that serve to hold the offering and to remind people of the power of sacrificial giving and to pray for Alabaster needs. She envisioned people coming to church and celebrating their gifts to the Lord by marching around the sanctuary and emptying their alabaster containers into one, large container. Through such offerings, she imagined churches, parsonages, schools, and clinics on the mission field being built, beam by beam, brick by brick.

Elizabeth passed the rest of her journey to Miami basking in the glow of that incredible experience. She felt that God had indeed answered her prayer and had given her beloved church a plan that would facilitate giving at home and provide for those much-needed buildings on the mission field. She arrived home excited and hope-filled.

She carefully wrote out the details of this new Alabaster giving plan and then whisked them off to the General WFMS office as soon as she could, convinced that the idea was from God and would bring glory to Him. But time always has a way of dimming enthusiasm and allowing vision to fade, and a year later she was wondering if she had made a costly mistake.

The letter she had just received from the Nazarene Headquarters proved that it was too late to turn back. The WFMS had just placed an order for $1,000 worth of Alabaster boxes, certainly a lot of money to invest in a new and untried idea. A little over a year had passed since that eventful train ride, and many letters and communiqués had gone back and forth between her Miami home and the Kansas City office. Fourteen months of hard work and preparation had laid the foundation for this day, and it should have been a day of rejoicing. Instead, Elizabeth couldn't shake a certain solemn, pious, and oh-so-tempting voice somewhere in her mind.

Now you've done it. You've gone to Kansas City, and the General Council is all excited about this idea. Today they have invested $1,000 of God's money in boxes that will never bring in $1,000 in offerings in return. What a shameful waste!

Elizabeth felt a rising tide of doubt well up within her. What if that voice was right? What if the church never recouped this money—money that could have been sent to the mission field? She began to sense a darkness enveloping her, and she couldn't shake it.

She quickly hurried into her bedroom, shut the door, and knelt beside her bed. "Lord," she began in earnest, "You know this is not my plan. It's Yours. I commit the outcome of Nazarene Alabaster giving to You." Then, just as suddenly as the darkness had come, it was dispelled. Elizabeth felt a new peace, a new faith that God was indeed behind this giving plan. Now she was sure that time would bear that out.

* * *

Time has, indeed, proven Elizabeth's fears groundless. Over the years, Alabaster offerings have totaled $54,864,131,* more than 54,000 times that initial investment. Her dream of "churches, parsonages, schools, and clinics on the mission field being built, beam by beam, brick by brick" has become a thrilling, God-honoring, life-changing reality. And who knows what Nazarenes will give during the next 50 years. Is it unrealistic to believe God for $100 million—or even a quarter billion dollars? I think not!

---

*Total for 1949 through September 1997.

Chapter 2

Building in the Shadow of a Casino
Sault Ste. Marie, Michigan, U.S.A.

by Curtis Lewis Jr. and Tim Crutcher

ALABASTER HAD A RATHER SCANDALOUS and shady past. The biblical account makes it clear. On the face of it, it was somewhat shaky ground for a church offering program, don't you think?

But then God has a way of bringing light out of darkness, meaning out of questions—often from the most unlikely places. There is something about this unlikelihood that fits quite well with Alabaster. A case in point is the Sam Mackety Memorial Church of the Nazarene in Sault Ste. Marie [SOO SAYNT muh-REE], one of the oldest cities in America, which is located in northern Michigan, United States, just across the border from a Canadian city of the same name.

As people leave the casino, many pass a small building that runs according to the laws of a completely different economy.

Most of the people who travel along Shrunk Road on the Checkerboard Native American Reservation, it is safe to say, are not going to church. For many of them, church may be the farthest thing from their minds. They are headed to the Kewadin [kuh-WAH-duhn] Casino, one of the many Native American casinos scattered throughout the United States. They come by the thousands from miles around every day to put their money in large metallic boxes in the hope that more will come out of the boxes than originally put in. A few people go away happy; the vast majority leave disappointed. Such is the nature of casinos. In fact, casinos are built by the money put into their shiny boxes.

Kewadin Casino

As people leave the casino, many will pass a small building that runs according to the laws of a completely different economy. This building, too, was built by people who put money in boxes, though most of these containers were much smaller than the ones used next door. But what happens to this money is quite different. This money has helped build a place where the returns far outweigh the investments, and those who leave disappointed are few if any compared to those who leave happy and fulfilled. Some rival casino? Hardly! No, this place is a Church of the Nazarene, so close to the casino that it is literally in its shadow.

Sam Mackety, a Native American, dreamed of planting a church for his own people in Sault Ste. Marie, but he died before his dream was fulfilled. God used his wife, Geneva, and the sacrificial giving of the people called Nazarenes to bring this dream to reality. A garage owned by Maggie Krull is where it began. Once the place was cleaned out, a small group of Native Americans began meeting for church. Conditions were not ideal, to say the least. The space was crowded; and during the harsh northern Michigan winters, the group had to huddle together in blankets to keep warm. Then this small but faithful band of Christians was discovered by Milton Hoose, then superintendent of the Northern Michigan District. Immediately, he started the process of organizing a Native American church-type mission.

One of the first priorities for the small group was finding adequate space in which to worship. A garage is certainly not the most conducive setting for worship, not to mention the fact that it is difficult to invite friends to church when you tell them

Sam Mackety Memorial Church of the Nazarene

they have to bring their own blankets! But because the church is a multicultural ministry of the Church of the Nazarene, it qualifies for a share of the 20 percent* of Alabaster funds that is allocated to such ministries in the United States and Canada.

The church found and purchased with Alabaster money a suitable piece of property right next door to the Kewadin Casino. Of course, that may not seem like the ideal place for a church either. But then Jesus was often accused of hanging

---

*The other 80 percent goes to projects in the six World Mission regions. No Alabaster money is used at international Headquarters or on the field for administration, promotion, or amortization of loans.

around sinners, even for that first Alabaster offering. And who knows if God may use the sight of a church to prick the conscience of anyone going to spend their time and money while engaged in less worthy pursuits inside a gambling establishment.

The site next to the casino had a small house to which a Work and Witness team, again with the help of Alabaster funds, connected a small chapel. Later, a mobile home was purchased, again with Alabaster funds, which sits next to the church and now serves as the parsonage. And the church began to grow.

Recently another lot adjacent to the church became available that would provide adequate parking and future expansion. In faith that such space would soon be needed, Curtis Lewis Jr., current superintendent of the Northern Michigan District, called Bill Sullivan, director of Evangelism and Church Growth in Kansas City. Again, Alabaster was there. On July 3, 1998, with the help of an allocation of $18,000, the church finalized the purchase of the property—thereby planting new seeds, the fruit of which God is even now beginning to bring forth.

Today the Sam Mackety Memorial Church is pastored by Russell and Eloise Kreml [KREH-muhl]. They and their steadily growing church are reaching out to their community and helping to change lives through numerous ministries, including Alcoholics Anonymous support groups, community events, and various children's programs.

There they stand, side by side, two buildings representative of two completely different sets of values. The one, far larger and more impressive, invites people to get rich quick, to take a chance, to trust in fate, but often leaves them disappointed. The other building was built from the ground up by generosity, by service, and by faith in the One who holds all provision in His hands and who never lets His people down. It could be said that both buildings are changing lives, that both buildings are affecting their futures in some way. But in a thousand years when both buildings are dust, only the works of one of those buildings will remain standing.

Interested in a long-term investment? Which one do you think is the better choice?

Chapter 3

Building upon Majesty and Tradition
Versailles, France

THE PALACE OF VERSAILLES [ver-SIE] is arguably the most impressive remnant of the monarchy in France. Its large, richly ornamented buildings set amid world-famous grounds situated just a few miles outside of Paris draw visitors from around the world. People come to gawk at the rococo ceilings and rich tapestries or stroll along the carefully laid out paths among the flower beds and musical fountain gardens. Built by Louis XIV, the palace stands as a striking testimony of the power, prestige, and wealth that once was wielded by the privileged few.

Just a few hundred yards away, around a corner, and down a narrow, one-way street stands another building. This structure is far less impressive but in its own right is just as important, perhaps even more so, than its famous neighbor. No mobs of tourists crowd its gates. No merchants sell wares emblazoned with its picture. No stern-faced attendants check to see if you've paid to get in. Distinguished from the neighboring buildings only by being shorter and fronted with a small garden, the building could easily escape the notice of any passerby. Its unassuming facade marks it as a church, and the fact that it juts against its neighboring buildings rather than standing alone marks it as a Protestant church. But that is all one could tell from the outside. It has none of the trappings of power or influence. But it is here, not down the road at the palace, that decisions are being made that will affect eternity.

Versailles Church of the Nazarene

The Evangelical Church of the Nazarene in Versailles, at 17 rue du peintre Lebrun (the street address), was purchased with Alabaster funds in the early 1980s to initiate Nazarene work among

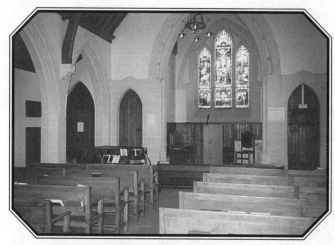
Sanctuary of the Versailles church

the native French population of the city—in addition to the Haitian and Cape Verdean populations of Paris with whom Nazarene work in France originally started. Actually an old Anglican chapel, the church is still adorned with beautiful, stained-glass windows illustrating the Beatitudes and dedicated to the memory of its parishioners from the World War I era.

Every Sunday, while the tour buses deliver their loads of tourists down the street, a small but growing group of brand-new Nazarenes gathers for worship. Their pastor, missionary Trevor Johnston, and his associate, Jean-Louis [ZHAHN-loo-EE], lead them through hymns and choruses that would be recognized the world over, at least for their tunes if not their words. Rev. Johnston preaches, and after the service most people linger for a cup of coffee or tea and the fellowship of believers.

On the surface, there is nothing unusual in all this. The scene could be repeated a hundred times over in a dozen different countries. What one does not see, however, is that none of these people—not a single one—would be here but for the Alabaster program of the Church of the Nazarene.

How nice it would be if all stories of missions and church growth were full of triumph and free of tragedy. But real life isn't like that, and neither, unfortunately, is the mission field. But then we serve a God who has always specialized in turning failure into success and crosses into empty tombs. One such empty tomb is the Alabaster church in Versailles.

The early days of the church in Versailles were ones of encouraging growth, especially for the difficult field of Western Europe. New people came to the church, and it was officially organized amid great celebration in 1988. A French pastor was appointed, and before long the church was averaging a respectable 60 people every Sunday. But then this pastor began to develop ideas contrary to Nazarene doctrine, which soon led to his leaving the church and taking over half the members with him.

In the wake of this tragedy, the missionaries moved to regroup and forge ahead. Another French pastor was appointed, and the small group of 20 continued to persevere. But this pastor, too, within a few more years left the church.

This was the situation in January of 1996. For over a decade, Nazarene missionaries and workers had labored in this place, one of the culturally most important areas of France. For that labor, nothing was left. No members. No attenders. Only a building, an empty shell, remained.

For that labor, nothing was left. Only a building, an empty shell, remained.

Missionary Trevor Johnston, who serves as district superintendent for France, had a choice to make. Questions nagged him. What to do now? Was this venture a mistake? Should they sell the building and recoup the loss? After all, there was the insidious voice, relentless and vexing: *What a waste! All the money spent on this building, and what good has it done? The money could have been used better elsewhere, perhaps to help the poor. All that sacrifice, wasted.*

However tempting it might be to listen to that voice, it would have been no more true in Versailles than it was in Bethany long ago—no more true for this Alabaster building than for that first alabaster jar. If there is one lesson Alabaster teaches, it is that in God's system of accounting, things are always more than they seem.

After much prayer and thought, Trevor decided not to sell the building. The building represented a commitment to the kingdom of God and the lost, searching people of Versailles. God wanted the Church of the Nazarene in Versailles, and that didn't change because the current situation was not exactly the original plan.

So in March 1996, Trevor began anew the work of the Church of the Nazarene in Versailles with nothing more than his family of four and a building purchased by the sacrificial giving of Nazarenes around the world. Adding this task to his heavy load as district superintendent meant that Trevor could not invest his full energies in rebuilding this church. It was all he could do to prepare for the services, make the hour-and-a-half round-trip from his home on the other side of Paris, and pray that God would send to the church those earnestly seeking Him. And that was exactly what God began to do.

At first, the services were attended only by Trevor, his wife, Mary, and their two sons, Andrew and Matthew. Occasionally, passing tourists would stop in out of curiosity; but they would not return. Then other people began to show up, drawn only by a building and by the hand of God.

One such person was Patrick, who found the church by mistake. He became a Christian through the evangelistic work of the Full Gospel Businessmen's Association. He attended a dinner in which businessmen shared their testimonies, and he accepted Christ as his personal Savior. His new Christian friends recommended that he find a church in his town of Versailles, but Patrick only knew of the Catholic churches and had no idea how to find an Evangelical church. Someone mentioned that there was a Seventh-Day Adventist church somewhere in Versailles, so Patrick went looking for it.

After driving around for some time on a Sunday morning, Patrick decided to park his car and set off on foot. Then he noticed right across the street a small church with a sign that advertised the Evangelical Church of the Nazarene. He had no idea who Nazarenes were; but since he was looking for an Evangelical church, and this one was immediately at hand, he thought he might as well take a look. He came to church that Sunday and has been coming ever since. Recently he has brought some of his friends as well.

Marie-Françoise [muh-REE-fran-SWAHZ] is a divorcé who felt God leading her back to church after an absence of years. Looking through the Versailles directory, she found a listing for an Evangelical church not far from where she lived and decided to check it out. There she found a small group of believers, a group that soon became her family.

That directory listing probably shouldn't have been there. The church ought to have closed when everybody was gone. But a building was there—a building that stood for a commitment. And so Marie-Françoise is now there as well.

Elizabeth has lived across the street from the church for a number of years. She took little notice of it, and she never felt compelled to attend. Like many, if not most, of her fellow French citizens, she was culturally Roman Catholic but gave little thought to God or church. Then she met Trevor one day as he was tending the small flower garden in front of the church. After a few such meetings, Trevor invited her to attend a Tuesday evening

Bible study. She has been faithfully attending and growing spiritually. As yet, she has not made a commitment to Christ, but there is much hope that soon she will.

Finally, an older Dutch gentleman we'll call Hans [HAHNZ] has just started coming to the church. Though he is married to a French Catholic woman and has spent the last several decades in France, his formative spiritual experiences occurred in Holland. Now, at a later stage of life, he is feeling the need to get back with God and get back into church. His wife's sister and her husband live on the rue du peintre Lebrun, and since the street is only one way, he had passed by this small church for many, many years. And when he decided to come back to church, he knew exactly where he would come. He knew none of the people, had read none of the literature, and attended no crusade or revival. All he knew was a building, and through that building he found the Church of the Nazarene.

God is at work in the city of Versailles. He is working in such a way that no one can doubt that it is His hand, not some human agency, that is growing the Church of the Nazarene there. He still requires the services of His faithful ministers. That will always be true. But here at least He has chosen to bring seekers into His fold, not through telephone contacts or large campaigns, but rather through the presence of a building—a building built through the sacrifices called Alabaster.

CHAPTER 4

Building on an African Hilltop
Mdantsane, Ciskei, South Africa

by Steve and Jean Hazelton
and Tim Crutcher

BUILDINGS DON'T BUILD THEMSELVES. That being the case, the Alabaster program would be rather ineffective if left to stand on its own. However, when it is combined with the forces of Work and Witness and the World Evangelism Fund, its effect can be profound indeed. One of the best places to see that at work is Zone 17 of Mdantsane township, Ciskei [SIS-kie], South Africa.

Mdantsane [mm-dahnt-SAH-neh] is a large suburb of the port city of East London beside the Indian Ocean. Ciskei, like its neighboring Transkei [TRANS-kie], used to be an independent tribal homeland. Since the creation of the new South Africa, however, the area has been reincorporated into the now unified country.

Spread out over the sprawling hills common to most of Ciskei, Mdantsane was divided into 17 zones during the apartheid era to make its overwhelmingly predominant Xhosa [HOH-suh*] resi-

---

*The first letter in the word *Xhosa* is the clicking sound used to get a horse to move faster.

dents easier for the government to handle. Now that apartheid is officially abolished, areas like this township are often more ignored than "handled," at least by those with political and economic power. The residents of Mdantsane fortunate enough to find employment (about one in three) usually find it in the businesses and industries common to port cities such as East London. But if money is being made in that city, it is not evident in Mdantsane, South Africa's second-largest township and one of its poorest and most crowded.

The streets of Mdantsane are awash with people. To drive through them is to face the twin hazards of streams of slowly moving pedestrians and lines of speeding taxi-vans. Women balancing on their heads live chickens, water buckets, or large bunches of tree branches pick their way carefully among the pressing throng of people and cars. Men, too, can be seen, their arms outstretched as they try to hail a ride from a passing car. And weaving their barefoot way along the dangerously narrow roads among the traffic and pedestrians are small groups of children with no one to look after them.

The houses that line these busy streets are as eclectic as the people who crowd them. One can see the traditional mud-brick, dome-shaped dwellings of the Xhosas. The passerby can also observe some small, well-built cement homes, the result of government reforms. And nestled among these structures, a person will occasionally find a nicer, privately built house. But many of the homes in

Mdantsane are hard-pressed to justify the name. Some of them, consisting only of clumsily assembled scrap metal, glass, wood, or cardboard, hardly look like houses at all. But if the shanties or shacks keep them dry, most people here won't quibble. It's far better than what lots of folks have.

In such situations of poverty and hopelessness, Alabaster sacrifices can make the greatest impact and provide the most hope.

Many of the people who live in Mdantsane are little better off than their homes. They cook their meals outside on wood fires—the fortunate ones on camping stoves—as the homes have no electricity or gas. They cook with water hauled from the nearby river or the only sporadically working city pumps. The lack of a sewage system also has an easily imagined effect. Many must scrounge for their food, and even as they eat the meal, they must think about the next one. In such situations of poverty and hopelessness as these, Alabaster sacrifices can make the greatest impact and provide the most hope. To see that, one need not look any farther than the Alabaster church in Zone 17 of Mdantsane.

This particular church began as a dream in the early '90s. In 1991 the church found a beautiful tract

Mdantsane Church of the Nazarene

of land on the corner of a hillside on Mdantsane's eastern edge. The site, prominently located at the top of a hill, looks over hundreds of homes in the area that leads down to the valley of the Buffalo River. Alabaster funds were requested and given for the purchase of the property and the materials needed to construct a simple, cement-block structure. When finished, the church could potentially seat 200 people.

The privilege of constructing this church was given to a Work and Witness team from the United States. They sent ahead of them an 8 x 15 x 8-foot metal shipping container with some of the Alabaster-purchased supplies and the equipment needed to complete the project. The team arrived

43

soon after and began the job. In their work, they demonstrated the love of Christ to the people of Ciskei. When they departed, they left behind a simple but solid gray building, a testimony to the cooperative work of Alabaster and Work and Witness, and a tangible reminder of Christ's sacrifice and of the generous giving of those who love Him. But that was not all.

A young Xhosa man named K. K. (short for Khayalethu Mangena) had no idea all this was happening just a few miles from the places he had found to lay his head. He was too busy trying to find something to eat and a place to sleep to think much about church. What little time he had after his basic needs were met was spent thinking, not of God, but of a special young woman whom he deeply loved.

K. K. had no money and no job—and no prospects for obtaining either. With unemployment among Xhosas in Mdantsane around 65 percent, K. K. knew that only the lucky could find work. He had tried going door to door, soliciting odd jobs in gardening, construction, or farming; but he met with little success. With no way to support a family, marriage was out of the question. And even if he should find a job, it would likely take him years to save up the money needed to pay the lobola [loh-BOH-luh], the bride-price owed in Xhosa tradition to the family of his future wife, in this case about U.S.\$1,000 or about seven months' salary. Without the lobola payment, marriage was not permitted.

The lobola is an important part of Xhosa tradition for two reasons. First, it proves to the bride's family that the young man has sufficient financial resources to take care of her. Second, it recompenses the bride's family for the money spent on raising and educating her. Plus, it is supposed to cover some of the income the family will forfeit in giving away a potential breadwinner. Losing such a family member can mean great economic hardship to aging parents living on their meager pension.

Faced with this situation, K. K. and his girlfriend decided to do what an increasing number of young Xhosa couples have done. They chose to behave as if they were married, even though they were not so legally and couldn't live in the same house. This practice is understandably frowned upon in Xhosa culture, but this couple didn't feel as if they had much choice.

This time was difficult for K. K. and his sweetheart. They had three children, one right after the other. Providing for these babies was a hardship, and K. K.'s prospects for employment had hardly improved. Then, soon after their third child was born, something happened in their lives to change them forever.

One Sunday morning, K. K. was invited to attend a service in a newly built church, situated near the top of a hill not too far from where he was living. There, in that simple church, K. K. found Jesus. He brought his young family to church, and his girlfriend also accepted the Lord as her Savior. But in the midst of the joy they had discovered in this newfound life and church family, they felt the conviction of the Holy Spirit. They knew they had to make things right with the Lord and become a truly married couple. But they still faced the problem of the lobola.

Before the wedding cake was cut, K. K. gave a vibrant testimony of how God had worked in their lives.

Such was the situation K. K. brought to his new friends, the Nazarene missionaries and pastor. After much prayer and discussion, they decided to offer the bride's family a smaller lobola that could be paid over time. The missionaries gave K. K. the opportunity to earn part of the money with various assignments, and there were some moneymaking jobs he could do for the church as well. K. K. figured out that he could offer his future in-laws about U.S.$300. The young couple hoped that this would finally allow them to marry. So, with much fear and trembling, K. K. approached his girlfriend's family with the alternative plan. Miraculously, the offer was accepted.

The wedding, the first one in this new church, was planned for a few weeks later. On a sunny Palm Sunday afternoon, the small sanctuary was packed with people. Many of them were friends and family members who had never attended the church before. The service, which was translated from English to Xhosa, went according to plans—except for one thing. K. K. got so excited that he kissed his wife even before the ceremony reached the usual place for this act to occur.

After the service was over and before the wedding cake was cut, K. K. gave a vibrant testimony of how God had worked in their lives and enabled them to come to this happy juncture. With tears rolling down his face, he described his life before Christ, how his wrong choices almost destroyed his most valuable relationships. Then he talked about finding the Church of the Nazarene and his new life in Jesus. Tears flowed freely in the audience, and the small church resounded with praise to God.

Once the couple was officially married, they needed a place to live together. The church voted to make K. K. their church groundskeeper and caretaker. With the high crime rate in the area and no parsonage on the church premises, the congregation needed someone on the property all the time. And this is where Alabaster made a second, somewhat unexpected, appearance.

Because housing is so scarce in Mdantsane, the church had kept the 8 x 15 x 8-foot shipping container, which much of the building supplies and equipment had come in. The church members fixed it up with doors and windows into a suitable dwelling. Although it lacked hookups for electricity or water, it was safe and fireproof. And it provided shelter. Then the church offered the small structure to K. K. as a permanent home.

K. K. in front of his home

K. K. and his family moved into their new house immediately and became faithful members of the church. K. K. also serves the church as worship leader and continues to assist his pastor in caring for the property. His wife is teaching Sunday School. And now K. K. feels that God is calling him to be a pastor.

This wonderful Xhosa family found a home, both spiritually and physically, because obedient Nazarenes gave generously in a love offering called Alabaster.

CHAPTER 5

Building Stable Foundations on a Desert Sea
Peru, South America

by Alfred Swain and Tim Crutcher

A N AIR OF PERMANENCE. A sign of stability. A sense of consistency. These are some of the things that the Alabaster giving program of the Church of the Nazarene provides mission fields around the world. Through investments in land and buildings, the Alabaster program enables churches, educational institutions, administrative centers, and hospitals in worldwide areas to have a stable and visible place out of which to do their ministry. These structures demonstrate the church's commitment to an area and a sense of being there for the long haul. Often these buildings provide an anchor point for identity as well. People can point to the building, rather than a tree or a tent, and say to their neighbors, "That's my church."

But no matter how solidly we try to build our brick structures, no matter how deep we lay our concrete foundations, we can never avoid the fact that we live in a world marked by impermanence, a world where change often seems to be the only constant. Everything made by human hands is temporary. Sometimes we are reminded of that in rather painful ways. In Peru, one of those reminders goes by the somewhat ironic name of El Niño.

Peru is one of the fastest-growing mission areas of the Church of the Nazarene. Roger and Mary Winans arrived in 1917 to plant the first Church of the Nazarene. The church has since spread all over northern Peru and is now reaching the central and southern areas as well. Throughout the vast Amazon River basin in northern Peru, you will find Nazarene churches filled with people won to Christ from animistic beliefs. There are now over 600 Nazarene churches in Peru on 14 districts and over 42,000 Nazarenes. Alabaster has been there from its inception, making a great impact on the churches in Peru, from providing land for a district center to materials for corrugated-aluminum roofs.

To make a trip to the north Peruvian churches in the town of Chiclayo [chee-KLIE-oh], you would probably travel through the great Sechura [say-CHOO-ruh] Desert. You might have to worry about your vehicle breaking down or having enough fuel to make that long trip. But one thing you would normally not have to worry about is rain. The Sechura Desert and the area that surrounds it is always dry. At the start of 1998, that part of Peru had not seen rain in 15 years.

Such dryness, while indeed making it more difficult to farm crops and maintain adequate water supplies, is not completely without advantages, not the least of which is that mud adobe bricks are an ideal building material. The clay is cheap, the work of making the bricks simple, and one really need not worry about having to waterproof. Many families, especially in the tribal villages of the Aguaruna [AH-gwuh-ROO-nuh] and Huambiza [wahm-BEE-suh] Indians, built their own homes out of such materials. Many Nazarenes built their churches in the same way.

And so it was a bit surprising to missionary Al Swain and his colleagues when they heard rain dancing on the roof of the new church in the fishing village of Parachique [pah-ruh-CHEE-kay] on the Peruvian coast. The evening service was about to begin, and the latecomers found themselves unexpectedly wet when they finally arrived at church. The rain increased during the service, and by the time of the benediction, the rain had built up to a heavy downpour. Missionary Swain and his team had no choice but to venture out in the suddenly soggy weather, as they had to be in Chiclayo that next day. They knew the going would be tough, but they never expected what they would encounter in the next few hours.

With water pouring over the road, the mission team made its cautious way forward.

One predictable feature of deserts is that whenever it rains, it floods. Ground unused to rain becomes so hard and impenetrable that it cannot absorb water, or at least not very quickly. This is a fact of geology (at least on paper), and the Sechura Desert is no exception. But that is scant comfort when one finds oneself in a new inland sea that didn't exist a mere six hours before.

The road through the desert was built up a bit from ground level, and so the missionaries found themselves traveling along a road that quickly became a dike, a battle line drawn with a huge new sea on one side and a vast open space on the other. And as the rains seemed to have no intention of letting up and the dike was made of little more than earth, the winner of such a contest is not difficult to guess. With water pouring over the road, the mission team made its cautious way forward. About midnight, however, the current of water became so bad that the missionaries' vehicle could go neither forward nor backward. If that wasn't bad enough, the flowing torrent had also begun to undermine the road itself. At that point, there was little to do but pray and wait.

After four hours of waiting in the complete darkness, the rain finally stopped, enabling the team to continue their journey. Half a mile later, the headlights of the car illuminated a raging river that had broken through the erstwhile dike and washed out over a hundred yards of the highway. Again with little choice and no hope of making it to Chiclayo, they turned their vehicle around to once

District Superintendent Modesto Rivera, missionary Dan Brewer, and two Sunday School boys at the Villa Hermosa Church in Chiclayo that was destroyed by El Niño.

again cross the flooded desert, making their way back through the unexpected, temporary sea after a 14-hour journey to nowhere.

The experiences of Al Swain and his team, nerve-racking and frightening as they were, were by no means the worst that the El Niño rains delivered that night and over the ensuing weeks. The desert became a sea 120 miles long and 30 miles wide. Bridges and roads were washed away throughout northern Peru. And 100,000 families watched helplessly as their adobe homes literally melted into heaps of mud. More than 200 Nazarene families were among them, and 20 Nazarene church buildings disappeared under the raging floodwaters that invaded the towns and villages, some of them washed away from land bought with Alabaster funds, some washed out from under Alabaster-purchased roofs.

So what does a church do in the face of such a loss? We feel with those who have lost their homes or even everything they had. But how do we respond tangibly? One could bemoan the loss of those Alabaster buildings and say, "What a waste! We know better than to invest our money in a place like that again." But then that would contradict what Alabaster is all about, wouldn't it? Church buildings are just an expression of what the church is all about; they aren't the church itself. And Alabaster exists to support the church, not just to build buildings for the sake of building them.

And so Alabaster is again hard at work in northern Peru. While Nazarene Compassionate Ministries has helped provide the temporary needs of those displaced and dispossessed by the devastating rains, Alabaster funds are being used to provide more, though by no means complete, help, just as they did almost 10 years ago in the face of a terrible earthquake. Alabaster moneys are the vehicle by which our love and concern and dedication to the gospel are transformed into flesh and blood—or rather concrete and mortar. In the past, Alabaster showed that the church was committed to being in these areas, and it continues to do so. And who knows, maybe that is just what God wants the non-Christians in these areas to see.

Upon sturdy and waterproof foundations, metal structures are being built that have a better chance of surviving future storms.

Of course, we would be foolish not to learn from the past. And so the new churches being reconstructed in Morrope [moh-ROH-pay], Lambayeque [LAHM-bah-YAY-kay], Ferrenafe [FEH-ray-NAH-fay], Tumbes [TOOM-behs], San Pedro [SAHN PAY-droh], and Chiclayo are following a plan of solid foundations. Upon sturdy and waterproof foundations, metal structures are being built that have a better chance of surviving future storms.

The Nazarenes of northern Peru are dedicated to their denomination. They have worked hard and will continue to do so to establish the church, both spiritually and physically, in their towns and villages. Through Alabaster, the church around the world has shown itself to be in partnership with Nazarenes, wherever they are. We understand that our buildings are not permanent, and we know that what happened in 1998 in Peru could happen again. We pray that it does not. But if it does, if El Niño strikes again in 10 to 15 years, the church will continue to demonstrate its commitment to northern Peru. And Alabaster will no doubt be waiting in the wings as an instrument of that commitment, a tangible reminder that even if the buildings we build are not permanent and everlasting, the gospel that is proclaimed within them is.

CHAPTER 6

Building on Good Soil in Asia
Indonesia, Japan, and Thailand

by Robert McCroskey Jr. and
Tim Crutcher

MOST OF US HAVE HEARD THE EXPRESSION "Give a man a fish, and he will eat for a day. Teach a man to fish, and he will eat for a lifetime." According to such logic, if you just meet someone's needs, the need will come back, and you may have to help again and again and again. However, if you empower people, if you help them help themselves, then their needs can be met, and you can then move on to help others—and eventually so might they.

The funds given through the Alabaster program of the Church of the Nazarene are often used like that. This type of Alabaster gift to a church, sometimes called *seed* money, is combined with the financial, physical, and personal resources of a given church to help them, not just to meet a need, but to lay the foundation for future needs as well. It isn't *rescue* money to help a floundering church. It's an investment in a growing church that may eventually reap 30, 60, or even 100 times what was sown. One exciting example of that is the Yogyakarta [YOHG-yuh-KAHR-tuh] First Church of the Nazarene in Indonesia.

The Church of the Nazarene planted its first church in Indonesia on the island of Java in 1977, when Robert and Linda McCroskey were sent there. Of course, God had already been there ahead of them and was preparing the way. First, He led a national pastor to them, one who was just graduating from a nearby nondenominational Bible school and who was looking for a church in which to serve. Then He led them to the eastern edge of town—so far out that they made it there before electricity did—to a house perfectly suited as a parsonage for the new pastor and his family. Then he led them to a haunted house.

The so-called possessed house was situated two blocks from the newly rented parsonage. Since nobody wanted to live there for fear of the ghosts and spirits, the owner was willing to rent it for literally pennies a month. The church leased the property for three years, cleaned it physically with soap and water, and dedicated it with prayer. Services were begun on Good Friday in 1977. Aside from the family of the pastor and the missionaries, one person showed up.

Through the hard work and sacrifice of the missionaries and the national pastor and his family, the church took root and grew. Within five years, they had to stack chairs on the front porch of that once-haunted-now-hallowed house to make room for all the people who wanted to come. They needed a new place to worship, but it would have taken a long time to save the money needed to purchase the land and build a church. Then Alabaster entered the picture.

During the next two years, U.S. $60,000 of Alabaster money was given to the Yogyakarta church to purchase land and to build a parsonage and a small church. Later, the property would also include a student center and a small dormitory for the soon-to-be Nazarene Bible College.

Without the help of Alabaster, this important milestone in church maturity would no doubt have taken much longer.

The Nazarene congregation, while only averaging 65 people on a Sunday, decided in faith to build a bigger sanctuary than they needed. The congregation knew their international church family was supporting them, but they also knew, with that support, came the expectation that the investment would be put to good use. Believing that God would indeed bless their work, they built a sanctuary large enough for 250 people, four times their current attendance.

The people's faith has proven to be well-founded, and the investment has been put to good use. Today, 14 years later, that church is financially the strongest one in the whole area. Averaging 325 in two services each Sunday, the church has been completely self-supporting for over 10 years. Without the help of Alabaster, this important milestone in church maturity would no doubt have taken much longer.

But the church has done more than just meet its own financial needs. It has also taken the lead in providing for the financial needs of others. They

Yogyakarta First Church of the Nazarene

have supported pastors in smaller churches in the area. They have helped and nurtured students at the Nazarene Bible College and consistently pay their educational budgets. They have also taken the lead in many nonfinancial areas of church growth and development.

In the manner in which they received, First Church of the Nazarene in Yogyakarta is now giving. And one day in the not-so-distant future, some of the churches they are supporting will be strong enough to support still other churches. And so the seed has taken root. And so the initial Alabaster investment bears new fruit, and it will continue to do so until the Lord returns.

* * *

Indonesia is not the only place in the Asia-Pacific Region in which one can see the growth of an Alabaster investment. Another incredible story of growth comes from the Japan District, a story that was almost 50 years in the making.

The property sold for several million dollars—almost 1,000 times its original value!

Soon after the Alabaster program was initiated and promoted, the generosity of Nazarenes around the world soon created a wonderful quandary. Where should that money first be spent? One of those first allotments in the early years of Alabaster went to Japan, where it was used to purchase a home in which William Eckel, pioneer Nazarene missionary to Japan, lived. The amount was about U.S. $5,000.

God blessed the work of Rev. Eckel and those who followed him in Japan. People came to know the Lord and His sanctifying power through that work made possible, in part, through the first Alabaster purchase. The church grew and prospered, and in 1979 Japan became a self-supporting, self-governing, self-propagating, regular district. Surely that would have been reward enough for that initial Alabaster investment. God had taken that sacrifice and used it to His glory. What more could be asked?

But God's abundant mercy and provision is never confined by the limits of our imagination, and He had yet more work in store for that first investment. When Japan became a regular district, the decision about what to do with the properties and assets of the district passed from the World Mission Division in Kansas City to the leadership of the Japan District. Realizing they no longer needed that original Alabaster property, the district leaders decided to sell it. And because real estate prices in Japan had skyrocketed, the property sold for several million dollars—almost 1,000 times its original value!

In 1988, upon learning that the Church of the Nazarene had an open door to begin work in the Southeast Asian country of Thailand, the Advisory Board of the Japan District voted to set aside a major portion of the proceeds from the sale of that Alabaster property to set up a trust fund. The interest from this money would be able to pay missionary

Parsonage in Bangkok, Thailand, the first property purchased

salaries and purchase some needed property. Thus, Nazarene work could begin in Thailand without any additional World Evangelism Fund (formerly General Budget) expense!

"Still other seed fell on good soil. It came up and yielded a crop, a hundred times more than was sown" (Luke 8:8, NIV). A better description of Alabaster would be hard to find!

CHAPTER 7

Building a Place Called Gratitude
Quezaltenango, Guatemala

by Leonel de Leon Vega and Tim Crutcher

ALL OF US LIKE TO GIVE GIFTS. Sure, receiving presents is nice; but parents, as well as many others, know the greatest joys of Christmas and birthdays are not those of getting but of giving. Those who understand that best can spend hours looking for just the right gift. And when such a gift is given, not much can compare with the grateful smile of a child or loved one getting "just what I always wanted."

The love of gift giving is one way we are like our Heavenly Father. Yet, while God is able to share and rejoice in every grateful thought and thankful prayer, often we are asked to give and then never get to share in the joy of seeing that gift thankfully received. If you've ever felt that way about your Alabaster giving, then let us tell you about a place called "A Miracle of Gratitude."

In the mid-1980s, Rev. Leonel de Leon Vega and his wife were ministering at the Second Church of the Nazarene in the important Guatemalan city of Quezaltenango [kay-SAHL-tay-NAHN-goh].

The church was organized in 1983 with 6 members, and the Lord had multiplied their numbers almost sixfold to 35 members just a year later.

God continued to bless the church with numbers as well as its influence in the community. Many people who did not even attend still considered Second Church of the Nazarene as "their" church. Through this, God opened new doors for ministry. But as the church continued to grow, they kept running up against a wall—literally! The space they rented for their worship services seemed to get smaller and smaller, and people were forced to crowd into the small building, sometimes lining the walls, in the warm, humid Guatemalan weather.

A sense of expectation moved among the people, but no one quite knew what it was all about.

And so the church began to pray. They interceded to God for property that would be adequate for their needs—though such a dream seemed impossible. They knew they didn't have enough money to buy a piece of land, and with most of the congregation being relatively new Nazarenes, they didn't know about such things as Alabaster and other offerings and projects. Yet they knew God was at work in their community, and so they prayed with ever increasing fervor.

During that time, missionaries Harold and Emily Ray were a part of the congregation. They saw that God was testing the faith of this young church; still they knew He would provide. They also knew that Nazarenes around the world were already giving to help their brothers and sisters in situations just like this.

One Sunday morning, the congregation gathered again for worship. Then Rev. Harold Ray arrived at church with something of an air of mystery about him. A sense of expectation moved among the people, but no one quite knew what it was all about.

During the worship service, as they were preparing to pray and lift their need to the Lord, missionary Ray stood up and said, "I believe it will not be necessary to pray for property anymore." Heads turned. The pastor and his people began to wonder. Sure, they knew of God's power and grace. They understood that He already knew about their need, and they believed He could fulfill it. But here was a missionary telling them not to pray! Rather strange, to say the least. As the pastor began to protest that they must continue in prayer, Rev. Ray told the congregation that the reason no more prayer was needed was that God had already responded.

Rev. Ray invited Pastor Leonel to join him at the front of the church. Then he handed the pastor a sheet of paper—the deed to a perfectly situated piece of property, one that the church knew it could never afford.

"Our church around the world has made provision for some needy local churches," Harold Ray continued. He then explained that the money had come from the Nazarene Alabaster Fund. He retold the Bible story of the woman who poured her sacrifice of perfume on Jesus' feet out of gratitude for

Property for "A Miracle of Gratitude" Church of the Nazarene. Pastor Leonel de Leon Vega is standing next to the sign on the left side. Emily Ray, founder and former pastor, is next to the sign on the right side.

what He had done. In memory of that act of love, the Nazarenes give to the Alabaster Offering out of gratitude for what God has done. Then Rev. Ray told them this property purchase was the direct result of that gratitude, paid from money Nazarenes around the world had laid at the Master's feet.

For the rest of the day Second Church of the Nazarene celebrated. They rejoiced to know that God had taken care of them, and they were profoundly grateful to their brothers and sisters whom God had used as His agents of provision.

Today there is a beautiful church building and parsonage occupying that piece of land. The members of Second Church have never forgotten that tremendous gift. In fact, to demonstrate their thanksgiving to God and the people called Nazarenes, they have named the property "A Miracle of Gratitude."

So, if you should ever find yourself discouraged, or if you ever wonder if the money you put in that small Alabaster box does any good, let your mind wander to Quezaltenango, Guatemala, one of hundreds of places where your gifts are very much appreciated. And if you should ever find yourself in Quezaltenango, you ought to see this "Miracle of Gratitude" for yourself. After all, without you, it wouldn't be there.

CHAPTER 8

Building More than Buildings
A Testimony of Diane Barker, Missionary to Australia

*T*HE REAL DIFFERENCE ALABASTER *makes is in people. It is perhaps fitting that the last chapter in this book is a story that shows that when we give to Alabaster, the ripples we create spread far and wide indeed.*

I was born after the dream of Alabaster had become reality. My father, who was in the military, saw to it that we attended Nazarene churches wherever we lived. Though he was not a Christian while I was growing up, my father had seen something in Nazarenes he had not experienced in other churches. No matter where we lived, we always went to a Nazarene church.

In 1962 my mom and siblings joined my dad in Okinawa [OH-kee-NAH-wuh], Japan. That experience brought my first awareness of missions. We attended Keystone Church of the Nazarene, which was a mission responsibility then. I still remember, via pictures, what the church looked like—masonry-block walls with holes for decoration. Doyle and Mattie Shepherd were the missionary pastors. The small church had many needs, but God was faithful to meet each one. And even though it was not built with Alabaster money (although Alabaster moneys assisted the church in later years), having a church in Okinawa brought home to me the importance of having church buildings in world mission areas.

Now that I'm a missionary, I believe that church in Okinawa and the Shepherds instilled a deep desire in me, as a young child, to later serve the Lord on the mission field. Without the church being there, I might have never listened to the Voice calling me, because I might not have been in a Nazarene church. That experience laid the groundwork for my learning what Alabaster was all about.

To me, Dot was Christ in skin. Her excitement of Alabaster remains with me to this day.

I was a young teen when Alabaster became a part of my life, and I learned to participate in giving with zeal. Our NWMS president, Dot Jakes, told remarkable stories of how others sacrificed around the world to build churches, hospitals, and schools. I, of course, remembered the Shepherds in Okinawa, so I had reality to draw from. Dot's stories were my stories. I can still remember a song we marched to when we received the Alabaster Offering. For some, it was just a song. But for me, I knew well that the coins and bills poured out of Alabaster boxes really did make a difference. I, too, could help—even in a small way.

Dot Jakes not only shared the stories and took the offering but also was a living witness to me of who Christ was. She shared herself in a way that I had seen no other person do. To me, Dot was Christ in skin. Her excitement of Alabaster remains with me to this day. I get excited all over again every time I'm with her. Today Dot is once again serving as NWMS president in Goodlettsville, Tennessee, the church I attended as a teen, and she is constantly sharing the Light with those around her. In a way, she represents what Alabaster is, not just what it buys: something beautiful being poured out for others.

Attending this same church was the visionary for Alabaster, Elizabeth Vennum, and her husband, Earl. I remember Mrs. Vennum telling of the vision God had given her to start the Alabaster program. I never tired of hearing her relive how God sent her the Alabaster idea. I guess because I had lived where an Alabaster church was needed, I could appreciate the dream in a different way. The main thing I remember was Mrs. Vennum's passion to share the gospel through the construction of buildings. She impassioned me to give out of that same love.

One day I realized I had done the unforgivable: I had failed to put any money in my Alabaster box, and two days later was Alabaster Sunday in our church. To me, this was a very serious matter. I was just 18, but I believed God used my small amount in a big way. I was a hairstylist, so I promised the Lord all my tips for the Alabaster Offering. That Saturday, the next day, I did extremely well. God had prompted others to be generous with me. I was not surprised, though, for He is faithful to our faithfulness. And that Sunday my Alabaster box had $30. It seems small today, but in 1977 it was more than a day's wage for some people.

But God still had more lessons for me to learn about Alabaster and the real meaning behind giving. When my husband and I were in college preparing to be missionaries, the time came for Alabaster giving again. Once again, Elizabeth Vennum stood and gave a testimony.

I realized Elizabeth was giving back an important part of herself and Earl to the Lord.

Rev. Vennum had to sell her home after her husband, Earl, died. Needing to downsize, she sold many of her possessions. One of those treasures was her china. That may not seem like such a big thing, but when you have been in a parsonage for many years and done a lot of entertaining, the china has many stories to tell. Elizabeth shared how God, one more time, asked her to help construct buildings for Him. She was to give all of her china money to Alabaster. I realized Elizabeth was giving back an important part of herself and Earl to the Lord. There was no hesitation in her voice, only pure joy that others might come to know the Creator and His love through this offering. She was willing to part with a cherished possession to see the Kingdom built. By Mrs. Vennum's example, I learned what all Christians should be willing to do—obey God completely. And I began to catch part of Elizabeth's passion.

Now I have served the Lord for over five years on the mission field. I have seen firsthand the marvelous results of Alabaster dollars and say, "Praise the Lord!" Alabaster is a fantastic program that is more than just a program. Without it, many missionaries will not have homes. Many people will die because there will be fewer clinics and hospitals. Many students at all levels—elementary, high school, and higher education—will not receive needed training and education. And many church congregations will have to meet outside.

And still there are churches right now in need of buildings. I visited a church that could hold 30 comfortably but had averaged 70 in attendance every Sunday. I've worked in a college that could not accept any more students due to a lack of space. I'm working at a college now that needs a chapel because the library, where they used to meet, is now filled with books.

I hope and pray that more people will allow God to bless them through giving to Alabaster. And the blessings, which are on both ends, reach far greater than any of us will ever know. The nickels, dimes, quarters, and dollars do actually help build a church or home or clinic or school. I have seen them with my own eyes. And I still love to parade in the Alabaster march when our churches have it—even on the mission field. Oh, I know it isn't just the amount God wants and needs; He wants and needs our obedience.

Dot Jakes and Elizabeth Vennum are beautiful examples of willing, obedient disciples. They taught me much about service to God; and if we could all catch their *mission*, their *vision*, we would see God's kingdom increase even more—through Alabaster.

Terry and Diane Barker, missionaries to Australia

Afterword

FACT: The line of people in the world, standing shoulder to shoulder, who do not know Christ as Savior would be 750,000 miles long, circle the globe 30 times, and grow 20 miles longer every day.

This sobering fact should motivate Nazarenes to give generously and selflessly to Alabaster so that centers of holiness evangelism can be built around the world. NOW!

Fact: Every day through the JESUS Film Partnership, hundreds of people are coming to Jesus.

This thrilling fact means more churches, parsonages, educational institutions, and clinics are needed. NOW!

Fact: The Church of the Nazarene in World Mission regions is growing by more than 10 percent annually. And in the United States and Canada, the greatest church growth is among multicultural groups.

This significant fact indicates that additional property and buildings are required. NOW!

Fellow Nazarenes, let's respond in love and obedience and give as never before to the Alabaster Offering in this 50th anniversary year. In so doing, God will use us—and our sacrificial gifts—to make an eternal difference.

—Nina G. Gunter
General NWMS Director